Look! We Have Come Through!

Shearsman Classics, Vol. 11

Other titles in the *Shearsman Classics* series:

1. *Poets of Devon and Cornwall, from Barclay to Coleridge*
　　　　　　　　　　　　　　　　　　(ed. Tony Frazer)
2. Robert Herrick: *Selected Poems* (ed. Tony Frazer)
3. *Spanish Poetry of the Golden Age,*
　　　in contemporary English translations (ed. Tony Frazer)
4. Mary, Lady Chudleigh: *Selected Poems* (ed. Julie Sampson)
5. William Strode *Selected Poems* (ed. Tony Frazer)
6. Sir Thomas Wyatt *Selected Poems* (ed. Michael Smith)
7. *Tottel's Miscellany* (1557)
8. *The Phœnix Nest* (1593)
9. *England's Helicon* (1600)
10. Mary Coleridge: *Selected Poems* (ed. Simon Avery)

12. D.H. Lawrence: *Birds, Beasts and Flowers*
　　　　　　　(with an Introduction by Jeremy Hooker)
13. D.H. Lawrence: *Studies in Classic American Literature*
　　　　　　　(with an Introduction by Jon Thompson)

Look!
We Have Come Through!

D.H. Lawrence

Shearsman Books

This edition published in the United Kingdom in 2011 by
Shearsman Books Ltd
58 Velwell Road
Exeter EX4 4LD

ISBN 978-1-84861-156-6

Look! We Have Come Through!
was first published in the United Kingdom in 1917
by Chatto and Windus, London; a US edition based on sheets from the
Chatto edition was issued by B.W. Huebsch, New York, in 1918.
A second, illustrated edition was issued by the Ark Press, Cornwall,
in 1958, and this was in turn reissued in the USA in 1959 by
The Rare Books Collection of the University of Texas.

Introduction copyright © Jeremy Hooker, 2011.

Contents

Moonrise	15
Elegy	16
Nonentity	17
Martyr à la Mode	18
Don Juan	20
The Sea	21
Hymn to Priapus	22
Ballad of a Wilful Woman	24
First Morning	28
"And Oh That the Man I Am Might Cease to Be"	29
She Looks Back	30
On the Balcony	33
Frohnleichnam	34
In the Dark	36
Mutilation	38
Humiliation	40
A Young Wife	42
Green	43
River Roses	44
Gloire de Dijon	45
Roses on the Breakfast Table	46
I Am Like a Rose	47
Rose of All the World	48
A Youth Mowing	50
Quite Forsaken	51
Forsaken and Forlorn	52
Fireflies in the Corn	53
A Doe at Evening	54
Song of a Man Who Is Not Loved	55
Sinners	56
Misery	57
Sunday Afternoon in Italy	58
Winter Dawn	60
A Bad Beginning	61
Why Does She Weep?	62
Giorno dei Morti	64
All Souls	65

Lady Wife	66
Both Sides of the Medal	68
Loggerheads	70
December Night	71
New Year's Eve	72
New Year's Night	73
Valentine's Night	74
Birth Night	75
Rabbit Snared in the Night	76
Paradise Re-Entered	78
Spring Morning	80
Wedlock	82
History	86
Song of a Man Who Has Come Through	87
One Woman to All Women	88
People	90
Street Lamps	91
"She Said As Well to Me"	93
New Heaven And Earth	95
Elysium	100
Manifesto	102
Autumn Rain	108
Frost Flowers	109
Craving for Spring	111

Appendix
(i) *Poems added to the section of the* Collected Poems *(1928) devoted to this book.*

Bei Hennef	117
Everlasting Flowers	118
Coming Awake	120

(ii) *Poems excluded from the first edition at the publisher's request*

Song of a Man Who Is Loved (revised version)	121
Song of a Man That Is Loved (1917 version)	122
Meeting Among the Mountains	123

Introduction

Look! We Have Come Through! is a book-length sequence of poems springing from D. H. Lawrence's relationship with Frieda von Richthofen, daughter of a German Baron, and, when they met, wife of Ernest Weekley, his former Professor of Modern Languages at Nottingham University College. It belongs to the period of Lawrence's life when he completed *Sons and Lovers* and wrote *The Rainbow* and *Women in Love*. While it is essentially about his relationship with Frieda, with whom he eloped to Germany in 1912, it is also strongly influenced by the death of his mother in 1911 and the spiritual crisis—sickness in mind and body—that followed. Lawrence's Foreword describes the poems as "intended as an essential story, or history, or confession", the critical experience occurring in the period of, "roughly, the sixth lustre of a man's life"—that is, from the age of 25 to 30. His Argument emphasizes the dramatic nature of the sequence. He speaks of "the protagonist" and of "the conflict of love and hate [that] goes on between the man and the woman, and between these two and the world around them, till it reaches some sort of conclusion, they transcend into some condition of blessedness". Foreword and Argument complement each other: *Look!* is both a personal confession and a drama. In both respects, it is closely related to the three novels which belong to the same period, 1912–1917.

Look! was completed in 1917 when the Lawrences (he and Frieda were married in 1914) were living in Cornwall. An outstanding feature of the poems is their dramatic immediacy. The couple's travels, and travails, between 1912 and 1916, included sojourns in places in Germany, Italy and England, names of some of which are appended to certain poems, enhancing the sense of immediacy. We cannot assume, however, that the poems were actually written during this period. As Mark Kinkead-Weekes writes, in the second volume of the Cambridge biography of D. H. Lawrence: "Sixty of the sequence we now read appear to date before Zennor but only twenty, or perhaps twenty-one, of these exist in versions earlier than 1917, and all but three of these have been substantially reconceived and in many cases transformed in the light of a later vision".

"*Look!*, then, is largely the product of "a later vision". It is not only the coming through of a crisis, but the working through. In this respect, Lawrence's famous Introduction to the American Edition of *New Poems* in 1918, which, he says, "should have come as a preface to *Look! We Have Come Through!*", is potentially misleading. There, he contrasts "the poetry of the beginning and the poetry of the end" with their "exquisite finality" with poetry of "the immediate present", and celebrates in Walt Whitman "the sheer appreciation of the instant moment, life surging itself into utterance at its very well-head". "Free verse", Lawrence says, "is, or should be, direct utterance from the instant, whole man".

The liberating influence of Whitman appears in a number of poems in *Look!* It does not dominate, however. The sequence is formally various, containing rhyming poems and ballads, reminiscences of Lawrence the Georgian, touches of Imagism, some Yeatsian symbolism, and even occasional lapses towards doggerel, as well as poems of Whitman-like utterance. In short, the modernism of *Look!* is that of poetry in transition between ages and styles. The unifying factors are theme and Lawrence's controlling voice.

If *Look!* is the poetry of "the instant, whole man", it is the poetry of a troubled man—and, in the context of our feminist age, a troubling one. Lawrence may eschew reminiscence, but he struggles under the burden of the past. The sequence not only begins where *Sons and Lovers* ends, with the protagonist in the condition of Paul Morel following his mother's death—"On every side the immense dark silence seemed pressing him, so tiny a spark, into extinction"—but is shadowed by that "darkness". In the astonishing 'All Souls' the man—clearly Lawrence speaking of his mother—says: "I am a naked candle burning on your grave". *Look!* is a death-haunted book. Its dark elements spring not only from Lawrence's response to his mother's death or even from the immense pressure of the war, conjoined to the Lawrences' embattled isolation, but from his wrestling with the death-in-life that he felt characterized modern civilization.

For all that, it is a vital book, informed by Lawrence's enormous creative energy. Both the crisis of the relationship and the threat of destruction contribute to the vitality, since Lawrence flamed most fiercely in opposition. Despite the "we" of the title, the directing consciousness is that of the man who is, in more than one sense, an oppositional figure. Behind him, we are aware of other Lawrence protagonists: Paul Morel, Ursula of *The Rainbow* with her "strange, passionate knowledge of religion and living", Birkin in *Women in Love*.

The protagonist of *Look!* seeks what Birkin seeks with Ursula: the balance of "two single beings, constellated together like two stars". As he says in 'Both Sides of the Medal', "we will learn to submit/each of us to the balanced, eternal orbit/wherein we circle on our fate/in strange conjunction". The idea of mutual submission plays alongside the submission the man requires of the woman.

Stars, moon, sun, river, sea, light, and darkness: whether in Germany, or Italy, or England, the places in the poems are located in a cosmic arena. As in the novels, Lawrence conceives his figures in relation to universal forces. With a heterodox religious sensibility, he draws heavily on religious language, transforming key Christian concepts and biblical myth into the terms of his own metaphysic. The man and woman are Adam and Eve. They "storm the angel-guarded/Gates of the long-discarded/Garden ('Paradise Re-Entered'). They reverse the roles of man and God: "Now in the cool of the day/it is we who walk in the trees/and call to God 'Where art thou?/And it is he who hides" ('Why Does She Weep?'). Real fulfilment is "our ratification,/our heaven, as a matter of fact./Immortality, the heaven, is only a projection of this strange but actual fulfilment,/here in the flesh' ('Manifesto'). The man, like Lawrence, is a preacher. Both of them, preaching to women, can be repellent. In these poems, though, the woman, far from being idealized as the weaker 'vessel', is herself a formidable fighter.

Look! is a fiercely oppositional book. The struggle, in love and hate, is between the man and the woman. The struggle is with family and with society, against the conventional mores in terms of which the lovers' relationship is condemned. It is against civilization, seen as corrupt, and comprehensively in need of renewal. Is there an element of class conflict in the fight between the miner's son and the daughter of a German Baron? More important, it seems to me, is Lawrence's rejection of 'love', as it is usually understood—the opposite of 'hate', and as a Whitman-like 'merging'—since it was his love for his mother, and hers for him, that had nearly killed him.

In *Look!* Lawrence, a great nature poet, is at war with nature. Frieda felt the deprivation of her children agonizingly, and Lawrence was tortured by her torment. He was afraid of losing her, while her yearning towards the children back in England militated against the conjunction of individual beings he was struggling to achieve. In *Look!* his resistance to nature takes the form of the man's attack upon mother-love—an emotional crux intensified by Lawrence's tie to his mother. In 'She Looks Back' mother-love is "destructive", "like a demon", "fierce as a murderess". The flower symbolism of the sequence affirms the priority of individual blossom over generative seed. In 'Rose of All the World' the man questions the woman: "The sharp begetting, or the child begot?/Our consummation matters, or does it not?" He answers by bidding the woman to: "blossom, be a rose/Of roses unchidden and purposeless; a rose/For rosiness only, without an ulterior motive". The temptation for a reader—W. H. Auden said Lawrence's love poems made him feel like a Peeping Tom—is to get involved, to take sides, and perhaps, on this occasion, as on others, to find the man monstrous in his egotism. This is a risk of poetry that is confession. It may also be a result of its immediacy, and of the sequence's continuing life. For *Look!* is an uncompromising book, completely focused on its subject, with no self-conscious seeking for sympathy from a reader. Here Lawrence, man and poet, utters the whole of himself.

Jeremy Hooker

Look! We Have Come Through!

Foreword

These poems should not be considered separately, as so many single pieces. They are intended as an essential story, or history, or confession, unfolding one from the other in organic development, the whole revealing the intrinsic experience of a man during the crisis of manhood, when he marries and comes into himself. The period covered is, roughly, the sixth lustre of a man's life.

Argument

After much struggling and loss in love and in the world of man, the protagonist throws in his lot with a woman who is already married. Together they go into another country, she perforce leaving her children behind. The conflict of love and hate goes on between the man and the woman, and between these two and the world around them, till it reaches some sort of conclusion, they transcend into some condition of blessedness.

Moonrise

And who has seen the moon, who has not seen
Her rise from out the chamber of the deep,
Flushed and grand and naked, as from the chamber
Of finished bridegroom, seen her rise and throw
Confession of delight upon the wave,
Littering the waves with her own superscription
Of bliss, till all her lambent beauty shakes towards us
Spread out and known at last, and we are sure
That beauty is a thing beyond the grave,
That perfect, bright experience never falls
To nothingness, and time will dim the moon
Sooner than our full consummation here
In this odd life will tarnish or pass away.

Elegy

The sun immense and rosy
Must have sunk and become extinct
The night you closed your eyes for ever against me.

Grey days, and wan, dree dawnings
Since then, with fritter of flowers
Day wearies me with its ostentation and fawnings.

Still, you left me the nights,
The great dark glittery window,
The bubble hemming this empty existence with lights.

Still in the vast hollow
Like a breath in a bubble spinning
Brushing the stars, goes my soul, that skims the bounds like a swallow!

I can look through
The film of the bubble night, to where you are.
Through the film I can almost touch you.

Eastwood

Nonentity

The stars that open and shut
Fall on my shallow breast
Like stars on a pool.

The soft wind, blowing cool
Laps little crest after crest
Of ripples across my breast.

And dark grass under my feet
Seems to dabble in me
Like grass in a brook.

Oh, and it is sweet
To be all these things, not to be
Any more myself.

For look,
I am weary of myself!

Martyr à la mode

Ah God, life, law, so many names you keep,
You great, you patient Effort, and you Sleep
That does inform this various dream of living,
You sleep stretched out for ever, ever giving
Us out as dreams, you august Sleep
Coursed round by rhythmic movement of all time,
The constellations, your great heart, the sun
Fierily pulsing, unable to refrain;
Since you, vast, outstretched, wordless Sleep
Permit of no beyond, ah you, whose dreams
We are, and body of sleep, let it never be said
I quailed at my appointed function, turned poltroon

For when at night, from out the full surcharge
Of a day's experience, sleep does slowly draw
The harvest, the spent action to itself;
Leaves me unburdened to begin again;
At night, I say, when I am gone in sleep,
Does my slow heart rebel, do my dead hands
Complain of what the day has had them do?

Never let it be said I was poltroon
At this my task of living, this my dream,
This me which rises from the dark of sleep
In white flesh robed to drape another dream,
As lightning comes all white and trembling
From out the cloud of sleep, looks round about
One moment, sees, and swift its dream is over,
In one rich drip it sinks to another sleep,
And sleep thereby is one more dream enrichened.

If so the Vast, the God, the Sleep that still grows richer
Have said that I, this mote in the body of sleep
Must in my transiency pass all through pain,
Must be a dream of grief, must like a crude
Dull meteorite flash only into light
When tearing through the anguish of this life,

Still in full flight extinct, shall I then turn
Poltroon, and beg the silent, outspread God
To alter my one speck of doom, when round me burns
The whole great conflagration of all life,
Lapped like a body close upon a sleep,
Hiding and covering in the eternal Sleep
Within the immense and toilsome life-time, heaved
With ache of dreams that body forth the Sleep?

Shall I, less than the least red grain of flesh
Within my body, cry out to the dreaming soul
That slowly labours in a vast travail,
To halt the heart, divert the streaming flow
That carries moons along, and spare the stress
That crushes me to an unseen atom of fire?

When pain and all
And grief are but the same last wonder, Sleep
Rising to dream in me a small keen dream
Of sudden anguish, sudden over and spent

Croydon

Don Juan

It is Isis the mystery
Must be in love with me.

Here this round ball of earth
Where all the mountains sit
Solemn in groups,
And the bright rivers flit
Round them for girth.

Here the trees and troops
Darken the shining grass,
And many people pass
Plundered from heaven,
Many bright people pass,
Plunder from heaven.

What of the mistresses
What the beloved seven?
—They were but witnesses,
I was just driven.

Where is there peace for me?
Isis the mystery
Must be in love with me.

The Sea

You, you are all unloving, loveless, you;
Restless and lonely, shaken by your own moods,
You are celibate and single, scorning a comrade even,
Threshing your own passions with no woman for the threshing-floor,
Finishing your dreams for your own sake only,
Playing your great game around the world, alone,
Without playmate, or helpmate, having no one to cherish,
No one to comfort, and refusing any comforter.

Not like the earth, the spouse all full of increase
Moiled over with the rearing of her many-mouthed young;
You are single, you are fruitless, phosphorescent, cold and callous,
Naked of worship, of love or of adornment,
Scorning the panacea even of labour,
Sworn to a high and splendid purposelessness
Of brooding and delighting in the secret of life's goings,
Sea, only you are free, sophisticated.

You who toil not, you who spin not,
Surely but for you and your like, toiling
Were not worth while, nor spinning worth the effort!

You who take the moon as in a sieve, and sift
Her flake by flake and spread her meaning out;
You who roll the stars like jewels in your palm,
So that they seem to utter themselves aloud;
You who steep from out the days their colour,
Reveal the universal tint that dyes
Their web; who shadow the sun's great gestures and expressions
So that he seems a stranger in his passing;
Who voice the dumb night fittingly;
Sea, you shadow of all things, now mock us to death with your
        shadowing.

Bournemouth

Hymn to Priapus

My love lies underground
With her face upturned to mine,
And her mouth unclosed in a last long kiss
That ended her life and mine.

I dance at the Christmas party
Under the mistletoe
Along with a ripe, slack country lass
Jostling to and fro.

The big, soft country lass,
Like a loose sheaf of wheat
Slipped through my arms on the threshing floor
At my feet.

The warm, soft country lass,
Sweet as an armful of wheat
At threshing-time broken, was broken
For me, and ah, it was sweet!

Now I am going home
Fulfilled and alone,
I see the great Orion standing
Looking down.

He's the star of my first beloved
Love-making.
The witness of all that bitter-sweet
Heart-aching.

Now he sees this as well,
This last commission.
Nor do I get any look
Of admonition.

He can add the reckoning up
I suppose, between now and then,

Having walked himself in the thorny, difficult
Ways of men.

He has done as I have done
No doubt:
Remembered and forgotten
Turn and about.

My love lies underground
With her face upturned to mine,
And her mouth unclosed in the last long kiss
That ended her life and mine.

She fares in the stark immortal
Fields of death;
I in these goodly, frozen
Fields beneath.

Something in me remembers
And will not forget.
The stream of my life in the darkness
Deathward set!

And something in me has forgotten,
Has ceased to care.
Desire comes up, and contentment
Is debonair.

I, who am worn and careful,
How much do I care?
How is it I grin then, and chuckle
Over despair?

Grief, grief, I suppose and sufficient
Grief makes us free
To be faithless and faithful together
As we have to be.

Ballad of a Wilful Woman

First Part

Upon her plodding palfrey
With a heavy child at her breast
And Joseph holding the bridle
They mount to the last hill-crest.

Dissatisfied and weary
She sees the blade of the sea
Dividing earth and heaven
In a glitter of ecstasy.

Sudden a dark-faced stranger
With his back to the sun, holds out
His arms; so she lights from her palfrey
And turns her round about.

She has given the child to Joseph,
Gone down to the flashing shore;
And Joseph, shading his eyes with his hand,
Stands watching evermore.

Second Part

The woman binds her hair
With yellow, frail sea-poppies,
That shine as her fingers stir.

While a naked man comes swiftly
Like a spurt of white foam rent
From the crest of a falling breaker,
Over the poppies sent.

He puts his surf-wet fingers
Over her startled eyes,

And asks if she sees the land, the land,
The land of her glad surmise.

Third Part

Again in her blue, blue mantle
Riding at Joseph's side,
She says, "I went to Cythera,
And woe betide!"

Her heart is a swinging cradle
That holds the perfect child,
But the shade on her forehead ill becomes
A mother mild.

So on with the slow, mean journey
In the pride of humility;
Till they halt at a cliff on the edge of the land
Over a sullen sea.

While Joseph pitches the sleep-tent
She goes far down to the shore
To where a man in a heaving boat
Waits with a lifted oar.

Fourth Part

They dwelt in a huge, hoarse sea-cave
And looked far down the dark
Where an archway torn and glittering
Shone like a huge sea-spark.

He said: "Do you see the spirits
Crowding the bright doorway?"
He said: "Do you hear them whispering?"
He said: "Do you catch what they say?"

Fifth Part

Then Joseph, grey with waiting,
His dark eyes full of pain,
Heard: "I have been to Patmos;
Give me the child again."

Now on with the hopeless journey
Looking bleak ahead she rode,
And the man and the child of no more account
Than the earth the palfrey trode.

Till a beggar spoke to Joseph,
But looked into her eyes;
So she turned, and said to her husband:
"give, whoever denies."

Sixth Part

She gave on the open heather
Beneath bare judgment stars,
And she dreamed of her children and Joseph,
And the isles, and her men, and her scars.

And she woke to distil the berries
The beggar had gathered at night,
Whence he drew the curious liquors
He held in delight.

He gave her no crown of flowers,
No child and no palfrey slow,
Only led her through harsh, hard places
Where strange winds blow.

She follows his restless wanderings
Till night when, by the fire's red stain,
Her face is bent in the bitter steam
That comes from the flowers of pain.

Then merciless and ruthless
He takes the flame-wild drops
To the town, and tries to sell them
With the market-crops.

So she follows the cruel journey
That ends not anywhere,
And dreams, as she stirs the mixing-pot,
She is brewing hope from despair.

Trier

First Morning

The night was a failure
    but why not?

In the darkness
    with the pale dawn seething at the window
    through the black frame
    I could not be free,
    not free myself from the past, those others—
    and our love was a confusion,
    there was a horror,
    you recoiled away from me.

Now, in the morning
As we sit in the sunshine on the seat by the little shrine,
And look at the mountain-walls,
Walls of blue shadow,
And see so near at our feet in the meadow
Myriads of dandelion pappus
Bubbles ravelled in the dark green grass
Held still beneath the sunshine—
It is enough, you are near—
The mountains are balanced,
The dandelion seeds stay half-submerged in the grass;
You and I together
We hold them proud and blithe
On our love.
They stand upright on our love,
Everything starts from us,
We are the source.

Beuerberg

And Oh—
That the Man I Am
Might Cease to Be—

No, now I wish the sunshine would stop,
and the white shining houses, and the gay red flowers on the balconies
and the bluish mountains beyond, would be crushed out
between two valves of darkness;
the darkness falling, the darkness rising, with muffled sound
obliterating everything.

I wish that whatever props up the walls of light
would fall, and darkness would come hurling heavily down,
and it would be thick black dark for ever.
Not sleep, which is grey with dreams,
nor death, which quivers with birth,
but heavy, sealing darkness, silence, all immovable.

What is sleep?
It goes over me, like a shadow over a hill,
but it does not alter me, nor help me.
And death would ache still, I am sure;
it would be lambent, uneasy.
I wish it would be completely dark everywhere,
inside me, and out, heavily dark
utterly.

Wolfratshausen

She Looks Back

The pale bubbles
The lovely pale-gold bubbles of the globe-flowers
In a great swarm clotted and single
Went rolling in the dusk towards the river
To where the sunset hung its wan gold cloths;
And you stood alone, watching them go,
And that mother-love like a demon drew you from me
Towards England.

Along the road, after nightfall,
Along the glamorous birch-tree avenue
Across the river levels
We went in silence, and you staring to England.

So then there shone within the jungle darkness
Of the long, lush under-grass, a glow-worm's sudden
Green lantern of pure light, a little, intense, fusing triumph,
White and haloed with fire-mist, down in the tangled darkness.

Then you put your hand in mine again, kissed me, and we struggled
        to be together.
And the little electric flashes went with us, in the grass,
Tiny lighthouses, little souls of lanterns, courage burst into an
        explosion of green light
Everywhere down in the grass, where darkness was ravelled in darkness.

Still, the kiss was a touch of bitterness on my mouth
Like salt, burning in.
And my hand withered in your hand.
For you were straining with a wild heart, back, back again,
Back to those children you had left behind, to all the aeons of the past.
And I was here in the under-dusk of the Isar.

At home, we leaned in the bedroom window
Of the old Bavarian Gasthaus,
And the frogs in the pool beyond thrilled with exuberance,
Like a boiling pot the pond crackled with happiness,

Like a rattle a child spins round for joy, the night rattled
With the extravagance of the frogs,
And you leaned your cheek on mine,
And I suffered it, wanting to sympathise.

At last, as you stood, your white gown falling from your breasts,
You looked into my eyes, and said: "But this is joy!"
I acquiesced again.
But the shadow of lying was in your eyes,
The mother in you, fierce as a murderess, glaring to England,
Yearning towards England, towards your young children,
Insisting upon your motherhood, devastating.

Still, the joy was there also, you spoke truly,
The joy was not to be driven off so easily;
Stronger than fear or destructive mother-love, it stood flickering;
The frogs helped also, whirring away.
Yet how I have learned to know that look in your eyes
Of horrid sorrow!
How I know that glitter of salt, dry, sterile, sharp, corrosive salt!
Not tears, but white sharp brine
Making hideous your eyes.

I have seen it, felt it in my mouth, my throat, my chest, my belly,
Burning of powerful salt, burning, eating through my defenceless
        nakedness.
I have been thrust into white, sharp crystals,
Writhing, twisting, superpenetrated.

Ah, Lot's Wife, Lot's Wife!
The pillar of salt, the whirling, horrible column
of salt, like a waterspout
That has enveloped me!
Snow of salt, white, burning, eating salt
In which I have writhed.

Lot's Wife! Not Wife, but Mother.
I have learned to curse your motherhood,
You pillar of salt accursed.

I have cursed motherhood because of you,
Accursed, base motherhood!

I long for the time to come, when the curse against you will have
    gone out of my heart.
But it has not gone yet.
Nevertheless, once, the frogs, the globe-flowers of Bavaria, the glow-
    worms
Gave me sweet lymph against the salt-burns,
There is a kindness in the very rain.

Therefore, even in the hour of my deepest, passionate malediction
I try to remember it is also well between us.
That you are with me in the end.
That you never look quite back; nine-tenths, ah, more
You look round over your shoulder;
But never quite back.

Nevertheless the curse against you is still in my heart
Like a deep, deep burn.
The curse against all mothers.
All mothers who fortify themselves in motherhood, devastating the
    vision.
They are accursed, and the curse is not taken off
It burns within me like a deep, old burn,
And oh, I wish it was better.

Beuerberg

On the Balcony

In front of the sombre mountains, a faint, lost ribbon of rainbow;
And between us and it, the thunder;
And down below in the green wheat, the labourers
Stand like dark stumps, still in the green wheat.

You are near to me, and your naked feet in their sandals,
And through the scent of the balcony's naked timber
I distinguish the scent of your hair: so now the limber
Lightning falls from heaven.

Adown the pale-green glacier river floats
A dark boat through the gloom and whither?
The thunder roars. But still we have each other!
The naked lightnings in the heavens dither
And disappear what have we but each other?
The boat has gone.

Icking

Frohnleichnam

You have come your way, I have come my way;
You have stepped across your people, carelessly, hurting them all;
I have stepped across my people, and hurt them in spite of my pare.

But steadily, surely, and notwithstanding
We have come our ways and met at last
Here in this upper room.

Here the balcony
Overhangs the street where the bullock-wagons slowly
Go by with their loads of green and silver birch-trees
For the feast of Corpus Christi.

Here from the balcony
We look over the growing wheat, where the jade-green river
Goes between the pine-woods,
Over and beyond to where the many mountains
Stand in their blueness, flashing with snow and the morning.

I have done; a quiver of exultation goes through me, like the first
Breeze of the morning through a narrow white birch.
You glow at last like the mountain tops when they catch
Day and make magic in heaven.

At last I can throw away world without end, and meet you
Unsheathed and naked and narrow and white;
At last you can throw immortality off, and I see you
Glistening with all the moment and all your beauty.

Shameless and callous I love you;
Out of indifference I love you;
Out of mockery we dance together,
Out of the sunshine into the shadow,
Passing across the shadow into the sunlight,
Out of sunlight to shadow.

As we dance
Your eyes take all of me in as a communication;
As we dance
I see you, ah, in full!
Only to dance together in triumph of being together
Two white ones, sharp, vindicated,
Shining and touching,
Is heaven of our own, sheer with repudiation.

In the Dark

A blotch of pallor stirs beneath the high
Square picture-dusk, the window of dark sky.

A sound subdued in the darkness: tears!
As if a bird in difficulty up the valley steers.

"Why have you gone to the window? Why don't you sleep?
How you have wakened me! —But why, why do you weep?"

"I am afraid of you, I am afraid, afraid!
There is something in you destroys me———!"

"You have dreamed and are not awake, come here to me."
"No, I have wakened. It is you, you are cruel to me!"

"My dear!"—*"Yes, yes, you are cruel to me. You cast*
A shadow over my breasts that will kill me at last"

Come!"—*"No, I'm a thing of life. I give*
armfuls of sunshine, and you won't let me live"

"Nay, I'm too sleepy!"—*"Ah, you are horrible;*
You stand before me like ghosts, like a darkness upright."

"I!"—*"How can you treat me so, and love me?*
My feet have no hold, you take the sky from above me"

"My dear, the night is soft and eternal, no doubt
You love it!"—*"It is dark, it kills me, I am put out."*

"My dear, when you cross the street in the sunshine, surely
Your own small night goes with you. Why treat it so poorly?"

"No, no, I dance in the sun, I'm a thing of life—"
"Even then it is dark behind you. Turn round, my wife."

"No, how cruel you are, you people the sunshine
With shadows!"—"With yours I people the sunshine, yours and mine—"

"In the darkness we all are gone, we are gone with the trees
And the restless river;—we are lost and gone with all these."

"But I am myself, I have nothing to do with these."
"Come back to bed, let us sleep on our mysteries.

"Come to me here, and lay your body by mine,
And I will be all the shadow, you the shine.

"Come, you are cold, the night has frightened you.
Hark at the river! It pants as it hurries through

"The pine-woods. How I love them so, in their mystery of not-to-be."
"—But let me be myself, not a river or a tree."

"Kiss me! How cold you are!—Your little breasts
Are bubbles of ice. Kiss me!—You know how it rests

"One to be quenched, to be given up, to be gone in the dark;
To be blown out, to let night dowse the spark.

"But never mind, my love. Nothing matters, save sleep;
Save you, and me, and sleep; all the rest will keep."

Mutilation

A thick mist-sheet lies over the broken wheat.
I walk up to my neck in mist, holding my mouth up.
Across there, a discoloured moon burns itself out.

I hold the night in horror;
I dare not turn round.

To-night I have left her alone.
They would have it I have left her for ever.

Oh my God, how it aches
Where she is cut off from me!

Perhaps she will go back to England.
Perhaps she will go back,
Perhaps we are parted for ever.

If I go on walking through the whole breadth of Germany
I come to the North Sea, or the Baltic.
Over there is Russia—Austria, Switzerland, France, in a circle!
I here in the undermist on the Bavarian road.

It aches in me.
What is England or France, far off,
But a name she might take?
I don't mind this continent stretching, the sea far away;
It aches in me for her
Like the agony of limbs cut off and aching;
Not even longing,
It is only agony.

A cripple!
Oh God, to be mutilated!
To be a cripple!

And if I never see her again?

I think, if they told me so
I could convulse the heavens with my horror.
I think I could alter the frame of things in my agony.
I think I could break the System with my heart.
I think, in my convulsion, the skies would break.

She too suffers.
But who could compel her, if she chose me against them all?
She has not chosen me finally, she suspends her choice.
Night folk, Tuatha De Danaan, dark Gods, govern her sleep,
Magnificent ghosts of the darkness, carry off her decision in sleep,
Leave her no choice, make her lapse me-ward, make her,
Oh Gods of the living Darkness, powers of Night.

Wolfratshausen

Humiliation

I have been so innerly proud, and so long alone,
Do not leave me, or I shall break.
Do not leave me.

What should I do if you were gone again
So soon?
What should I look for?
Where should I go?
What should I be, I myself,
"I"?
What would it mean, this
I?

Do not leave me.

What should I think of death?
If I died, it would not be you:
It would be simply the same
Lack of you.
The same want, life or death,
Unfulfilment,
The same insanity of space
You not there for me.

Think, I daren't die
For fear of the lack in death.
And I daren't live.

Unless there were a morphine or a drug.

I would bear the pain.
But always, strong, unremitting
It would make me not me.
The thing with my body that would go on living
Would not be me.
Neither life nor death could help.

Think, I couldn't look towards death
Nor towards the future:
Only not look.
Only myself
Stand still and bind and blind myself.

God, that I have no choice!
That my own fulfilment is up against me
Timelessly!
The burden of self-accomplishment!
The charge of fulfilment!
And God, that she is *necessary*!
Necessary, and I have no choice!

Do not leave me.

A Young Wife

The pain of loving you
Is almost more than I can bear.

I walk in fear of you.
The darkness starts up where
You stand, and the night comes through
Your eyes when you look at me.

Ah never before did I see
The shadows that live in the sun!

Now every tall glad tree
Turns round its back to the sun
And looks down on the ground, to see
The shadow it used to shun.

At the foot of each glowing thing
A night lies looking up.

Oh, and I want to sing
And dance, but I can't lift up
My eyes from the shadows: dark
They lie spilt round the cup.

What is it?—Hark

The faint fine seethe in the air!
Like the seething sound in a shell
It is death still seething where
The wild-flower shakes its bell
And the sky lark twinkles blue

The pain of loving you
Is almost more than I can bear.

Green

The dawn was apple-green,
    The sky was green wine held up in the sun,
The moon was a golden petal between.

She opened her eyes, and green
    They shone, clear like flowers undone
For the first time, now for the first time seen.

Icking

River Roses

By the Isar, in the twilight
We were wandering and singing,
By the Isar, in the evening
We climbed the huntsman's ladder and sat swinging
In the fir-tree overlooking the marshes,
While river met with river, and the ringing
Of their pale-green glacier water filled the evening.

By the Isar, in the twilight
We found the dark wild roses
Hanging red at the river; and simmering
Frogs were singing, and over the river closes
Was savour of ice and of roses; and glimmering
Fear was abroad. We whispered: "No one knows us.
Let it be as the snake disposes
Here in this simmering marsh."

Kloster Schaeftlarn

Gloire de Dijon

When she rises in the morning
I linger to watch her;
She spreads the bath-cloth underneath the window
And the sunbeams catch her
Glistening white on the shoulders,
While down her sides the mellow
Golden shadow glows as
She stoops to the sponge, and her swung breasts
Sway like full-blown yellow
Gloire de Dijon roses.

She drips herself with water, and her shoulders
Glisten as silver, they crumple up
Like wet and falling roses, and I listen
For the sluicing of their rain-dishevelled petals.
In the window full of sunlight
Concentrates her golden shadow
Fold on fold, until it glows as
Mellow as the glory roses.

Icking

Roses on the Breakfast Table

Just a few of the roses we gathered from the Isar
Are fallen, and their mauve-red petals on the cloth
Float like boats on a river, while other
Roses are ready to fall, reluctant and loth.

She laughs at me across the table, saying
I am beautiful. I look at the rumpled young roses
And suddenly realise, in them as in me,
How lovely the present is that this day discloses.

I Am Like a Rose

I am myself at last; now I achieve
My very self. I, with the wonder mellow,
Full of fine warmth, I issue forth in clear
And single me, perfected from my fellow.

Here I am all myself. No rose-bush heaving
Its limpid sap to culmination, has brought
Itself more sheer and naked out of the green
In stark-clear roses, than I to myself am brought.

Rose of All the World

I am here myself; as though this heave of effort
At starting other life, fulfilled my own:
Rose-leaves that whirl in colour round a core
Of seed-specks kindled lately and softly blown

By all the blood of the rose-bush into being —
Strange, that the urgent will in me, to set
My mouth on hers in kisses, and so softly
To bring together two strange sparks, beget

Another life from our lives, so should send
The innermost fire of my own dim soul out-spinning
And whirling in blossom of flame and being upon me!
That my completion of manhood should be the beginning

Another life from mine! For so it looks.
The seed is purpose, blossom accident.
The seed is all in all, the blossom lent
To crown the triumph of this new descent.

Is that it, woman? Does it strike you so?
The Great Breath blowing a tiny seed of fire
Fans out your petals for excess of flame,
Till all your being smokes with fine desire?

Or are we kindled, you and I, to be
One rose of wonderment upon the tree
Of perfect life, and is our possible seed
But the residuum of the ecstasy?

How will you have it?—the rose is all in all,
Or the ripe rose-fruits of the luscious fall?
The sharp begetting, or the child begot?
Our consummation matters, or does it not?

To me it seems the seed is just left over
From the red rose-flowers' fiery transience;

Just orts and slarts; berries that smoulder in the bush
Which burnt just now with marvellous immanence.

Blossom, my darling, blossom, be a rose
Of roses unchidden and purposeless; a rose
For rosiness only, without an ulterior motive;
For me it is more than enough if the flower unclose.

A Youth Mowing

There are four men mowing down by the Isar;
I can hear the swish of the scythe-strokes, four
Sharp breaths taken: yea, and I
Am sorry for what's in store.

The first man out of the four that's mowing
Is mine, I claim him once and for all;
Though it's sorry I am, on his young feet, knowing
None of the trouble he's led to stall.

As he sees me bringing the dinner, he lifts
His head as proud as a deer that looks
Shoulder-deep out of the corn; and wipes
His scythe-blade bright, unhooks

The scythe-stone and over the stubble to me.
Lad, thou hast gotten a child in me,
Laddie, a man thou'lt ha'e to be,
Yea, though I'm sorry for thee.

Quite Forsaken

What pain, to wake and miss you!
    To wake with a tightened heart,
And mouth reaching forward to kiss you!

This then at last is the dawn, and the bell
    Clanging at the farm! Such bewilderment
Comes with the sight of the room, I cannot tell.

It is raining. Down the half-obscure road
    Four labourers pass with their scythes
Dejectedly;—a huntsman goes by with his load:

A gun, and a bunched-up deer, its four little feet
    Clustered dead. And this is the dawn
For which I wanted the night to retreat!

Forsaken and Forlorn

The house is silent, it is late at night, I am alone.
                    From the balcony
          I can hear the Isar moan,
               Can see the white
Rift of the river eerily, between the pines, under a sky of stone.

Some fireflies drift through the middle air
                  Tinily.
     I wonder where
Ends this darkness that annihilates me.

Fireflies in the Corn

She speaks.
Look at the little darlings in the corn!
    The rye is taller than you, who think yourself
So high and mighty: look how the heads are borne
    Dark and proud on the sky, like a number of knights
Passing with spears and pennants and manly scorn.

Knights indeed!—much knight I know will ride
    With his head held high-serene against the sky!
Limping and following rather at my side
    Moaning for me to love him!—Oh darling rye
How I adore you for your simple pride!

And the dear, dear fireflies wafting in between
    And over the swaying corn-stalks, just above
All the dark-feathered helmets, like little green
    Stars come low and wandering here for love
Of these dark knights, shedding their delicate sheen!

I thank you I do, you happy creatures, you dears
    Riding the air, and carrying all the time
Your little lanterns behind you! Ah, it cheers
    My soul to see you settling and trying to climb
The corn-stalks, tipping with fire the spears.

All over the dim corn's motion, against the blue
    Dark sky of night, a wandering glitter, a swarm
Of questing brilliant souls going out with their true
    Proud knights to battle! Sweet, how I warm
My poor, my perished soul with the sight of you!

A Doe at Evening

As I went through the marshes
a doe sprang out of the corn
and flashed up the hill-side
leaving her fawn.

On the sky-line
she moved round to watch,
she pricked a fine black blotch
on the sky.

I looked at her
and felt her watching;
I became a strange being.
Still, I had my right to be there with her.

Her nimble shadow trotting
along the sky-line, she
put back her fine, level-balanced head.
And I knew her.

Ah yes, being male, is not my head hard-balanced, antlered?
Are not my haunches light?
Has she not fled on the same wind with me?
Does not my fear cover her fear?

Irschenhausen

Song of a Man Who Is Not Loved

The space of the world is immense, before me and around me;
If I turn quickly, I am terrified, feeling space surround me;
Like a man in a boat on very clear, deep water, space frightens and
        confounds me.

I see myself isolated in the universe, and wonder
What effect I can have. My hands wave under
The heavens like specks of dust that are floating asunder.

I hold myself up, and feel a big wind blowing
Me like a gadfly into the dusk, without my knowing
Whither or why or even how I am going.

So much there is outside me, so infinitely
Small am I, what matter if minutely
I beat my way, to be lost immediately?

How shall I flatter myself that I can do
Anything in such immensity? I am too
Little to count in the wind that drifts me through.

Glashütte

Sinners

The big mountains sit still in the afternoon light
    Shadows in their lap;
The bees roll round in the wild-thyme with delight.

We sitting here among the cranberries
    So still in the gap
Of rock, distilling our memories

Are sinners! Strange! The bee that blunders
    Against me goes off with a laugh.
A squirrel cocks his head on the fence, and wonders

What about sin?—For, it seems
    The mountains have
No shadow of us on their snowy forehead of dreams

As they ought to have. They rise above us
    Dreaming
For ever. One even might think that they love us.

Little red cranberries cheek to cheek,
Two great dragon-flies wrestling;
You, with your forehead nestling
Against me, and bright peak shining to peak—

There's a love-song for you!—Ah, if only
    There were no teeming
Swarms of mankind in the world, and we were less lonely!

Mayrhofen

Misery

Out of this oubliette between the mountains
five valleys go, five passes like gates;
three of them black in shadow, two of them bright
with distant sunshine;
and sunshine fills one high valley bed,
green grass shining, and little white houses
like quartz crystals,
little, but distinct a way off.

Why don't I go?
Why do I crawl about this pot, this oubliette,
stupidly?
Why don't I go?

But where?
If I come to a pine-wood, I can't say
Now I am arrived!
What are so many straight trees to me!

Sterzing

Sunday Afternoon in Italy

The man and the maid go side by side
With an interval of space between;
And his hands are awkward and want to hide,
She braves it out since she must be seen.

When some one passes he drops his head
Shading his face in his black felt hat,
While the hard girl hardens; nothing is said,
There is nothing to wonder or cavil at.

Alone on the open road again
With the mountain snows across the lake
Flushing the afternoon, they are uncomfortable,
The loneliness daunts them, their stiff throats ache.

And he sighs with relief when she parts from him;
Her proud head held in its black silk scarf
Gone under the archway, home, he can join
The men that lounge in a group on the wharf.

His evening is a flame of wine
Among the eager, cordial men.
And she with her women hot and hard
Moves at her ease again.

> *She is marked, she is singled out*
>   *For the fire:*
> *The brand is upon him, look you,*
>   *Of desire.*
>
> *They are chosen, ah, they are fated*
>   *For the fight!*
> *Champion her, all you women! Men, menfolk*
>   *Hold him your light!*
>
> *Nourish her, train her, harden her*
>   *Women all!*

Fold him, be good to him, cherish him
    Men, ere he fall.

Women, another champion!
    This, men, is yours!
Wreathe and enlap and anoint them
    Behind separate doors.

Gargnano

Winter Dawn

Green star Sirius
Dribbling over the lake;
The stars have gone so far on their road,
Yet we're awake!

Without a sound
The new young year comes in
And is half-way over the lake.
We must begin

Again. This love so full
Of hate has hurt us so,
We lie side by side
Moored—but no,

Let me get up
And wash quite clean
Of this hate.—
So green

The great star goes!
I am washed quite clean,
Quite clean of it all.
But e'en

So cold, so cold and clean
Now the hate is gone!
It is all no good,
I am chilled to the bone

Now the hate is gone;
There is nothing left;
I am pure like bone,
Of all feeling bereft.

A Bad Beginning

The yellow sun steps over the mountain-top
And falters a few short steps across the lake—
Are you awake?

See, glittering on the milk-blue, morning lake
They are laying the golden racing-track of the sun;
The day has begun.

The sun is in my eyes, I must get up.
I want to go, there's a gold road blazes before
My breast—which is so sore.

What?—your throat is bruised, bruised with my kisses?
Ah, but if I am cruel what then are you?
I am bruised right through.

What if I love you!—This misery
Of your dissatisfaction and misprision
Stupefies me.

Ah yes, your open arms! Ah yes, ah yes,
You would take me to your breast!—But no,
You should come to mine,
It were better so.

Here I am—get up and come to me!
Not as a visitor either, nor a sweet
And winsome child of innocence; nor
As an insolent mistress telling my pulse's beat.

Come to me like a woman coming home
To the man who is her husband, all the rest
Subordinate to this, that he and she
Are joined together for ever, as is best.

Behind me on the lake I hear the steamer drumming
From Austria. There lies the world, and here
Am I. Which way are you coming?

Why Does She Weep?

Hush then
why do you cry?
It's you and me
the same as before.

If you hear a rustle
it's only a rabbit
gone back to his hole
in a bustle.

If something stirs in the branches
overhead, it will be a squirrel moving
uneasily, disturbed by the stress
of our loving.

Why should you cry then?
Are you afraid of God
in the dark?

I'm not afraid of God.
Let him come forth.
If he is hiding in the cover
let him come forth.

Now in the cool of the day
it is we who walk in the trees
and call to God "Where art thou?"
And it is he who hides.

Why do you cry?
My heart is bitter.
Let God come forth to justify
himself now.

Why do you cry?
Is it Wehmut, ist dir weh?
Weep then, yea
for the abomination of our old righteousness.

We have done wrong
many times;
but this time we begin to do right.

Weep then, weep
for the abomination of our past righteousness.
God will keep
hidden, he won't come forth.

Giorno dei Morti

Along the avenue of cypresses
All in their scarlet cloaks, and surplices
Of linen go the chanting choristers,
The priests in gold and black, the villagers . . .

And all along the path to the cemetery
The round dark heads of men crowd silently,
And black-scarved faces of women-folk, wistfully
Watch at the banner of death, and the mystery.

And at the foot of a grave a father stands
With sunken head, and forgotten, folded hands;
And at the foot of a grave a mother kneels
With pale shut face, nor either hears nor feels

The coming of the chanting choristers
Between the avenue of cypresses,
The silence of the many villagers,
The candle-flames beside the surplices.

All Souls

They are chanting now the service of All the Dead
And the village folk outside in the burying ground
Listen—except those who strive with their dead,
Reaching out in anguish, yet unable quite to touch them:
Those villagers isolated at the grave
Where the candles burn in the daylight, and the painted wreaths
Are propped on end, there, where the mystery starts.

The naked candles burn on every grave.
On your grave, in England, the weeds grow.

But I am your naked candle burning,
And that is not your grave, in England,
The world is your grave.
And my naked body standing on your grave
Upright towards heaven is burning off to you
Its flame of life, now and always, till the end.

It is my offering to you; every day is All Souls' Day.

I forget you, have forgotten you.
I am busy only at my burning,
I am busy only at my life.
But my feet are on your grave, planted.
And when I lift my face, it is a flame that goes up
To the other world, where you are now.
But I am not concerned with you.
     I have forgotten you.

I am a naked candle burning on your grave.

Lady Wife

Ah yes, I know you well, a sojourner
    At the hearth;
I know right well the marriage ring you wear,
    And what it's worth.

The angels came to Abraham, and they stayed
    In his house awhile;
So you to mine, I imagine; yes, happily
    Condescend to be vile.

I see you all the time, you bird-blithe, lovely
    Angel in disguise.
I see right well how I ought to be grateful,
    Smitten with reverent surprise.

Listen, I have no use
    For so rare a visit;
Mine is a common devil's
    Requisite.

Rise up and go, I have no use for you
    And your blithe, glad mien.
No angels here, for me no goddesses,
    Nor any Queen.

Put ashes on your head, put sackcloth on
    And learn to serve.
You have fed me with your sweetness, now I am sick,
    As I deserve.

Queens, ladies, angels, women rare,
    I have had enough.
Put sackcloth on, be crowned with powdery ash,
    Be common stuff.

And serve now woman, serve, as a woman should,
    Implicitly.

Since I must serve and struggle with the imminent
    Mystery.

Serve then, I tell you, add your strength to mine
    Take on this doom.
What are you by yourself, do you think, and what
    The mere fruit of your womb?

What is the fruit of your womb then, you mother, you queen,
    When it falls to the ground?
Is it more than the apples of Sodom you scorn so, the men
    Who abound?

Bring forth the sons of your womb then, and put them
    Into the fire
Of Sodom that covers the earth; bring them forth
    From the womb of your precious desire.

You woman most holy, you mother, you being beyond
    Question or diminution,
Add yourself up, and your seed, to the nought
    Of your last solution.

Both Sides of the Medal

And because you love me
think you you do not hate me?
Ha, since you love me
to ecstasy
it follows you hate me to ecstasy.

Because when you hear me
go down the road outside the house
you must come to the window to watch me go,
do you think it is pure worship?

Because, when I sit in the room,
here, in my own house,
and you want to enlarge yourself with this friend of mine,
such a friend as he is,
yet you cannot get beyond your awareness of me
you are held back by my being in the same world with you,
do you think it is bliss alone?
sheer harmony?

No doubt if I were dead, you must
reach into death after me,
but would not your hate reach even more madly than your love?
your impassioned, unfinished hate?

Since you have a passion for me,
as I for you,
does not that passion stand in your way like a Balaam's ass?
and am I not Balaam's ass
golden-mouthed occasionally?
But mostly, do you not detest my bray?

Since you are confined in the orbit of me
do you not loathe the confinement?
Is not even the beauty and peace of an orbit
an intolerable prison to you,
as it is to everybody?

But we will learn to submit
each of us to the balanced, eternal orbit
wherein we circle on our fate
in strange conjunction.

What is chaos, my love?
It is not freedom.
A disarray of falling stars coming to nought.

Loggerheads

Please yourself how you have it.
Take my words, and fling
Them down on the counter roundly;
See if they ring.

Sift my looks and expressions,
And see what proportion there is
Of sand in my doubtful sugar
Of verities.

Have a real stock-taking
Of my manly breast;
Find out if I'm sound or bankrupt,
Or a poor thing at best.

For I am quite indifferent
To your dubious state,
As to whether you've found a fortune
In me, or a flea-bitten fate.

Make a good investigation
Of all that is there,
And then, if it's worth it, be grateful—
If not then despair.

If despair is our portion
Then let us despair.
Let us make for the weeping willow.
I don't care.

December Night

Take off your cloak and your hat
And your shoes, and draw up at my hearth
Where never woman sat.

I have made the fire up bright;
Let us leave the rest in the dark
And sit by firelight.

The wine is warm in the hearth;
The flickers come and go.
I will warm your feet with kisses
Until they glow.

New Year's Eve

There are only two things now,
The great black night scooped out
And this fire-glow.

This fire-glow, the core,
And we the two ripe pips
That are held in store.

Listen, the darkness rings
As it circulates round our fire.
Take off your things.

Your shoulders, your bruised throat!
Your breasts, your nakedness!
This fiery coat!

As the darkness flickers and dips,
As the firelight falls and leaps
From your feet to your lips!

New Year's Night

Now you are mine, to-night at last I say it;
You're a dove I have bought for sacrifice,
And to-night I slay it.

Here in my arms my naked sacrifice!
Death, do you hear, in my arms I am bringing
My offering, bought at great price.

She's a silvery dove worth more than all I've got.
Now I offer her up to the ancient, inexorable God,
Who knows me not.

Look, she's a wonderful dove, without blemish or spot!
I sacrifice all in her, my last of the world,
Pride, strength, all the lot.

All, all on the altar! And death swooping down
Like a falcon. 'Tis God has taken the victim;
I have won my renown.

Valentine's Night

You shadow and flame,
You interchange,
You death in the game!

Now I gather you up,
Now I put you back
Like a poppy in its cup.

And so, you are a maid
Again, my darling, but new,
Unafraid.

My love, my blossom, a child
Almost! The flower in the bud
Again, undefiled.

And yet, a woman, knowing
All, good, evil, both
In one blossom blowing.

Birth Night

This fireglow is a red womb
In the night, where you're folded up
On your doom.

And the ugly, brutal years
Are dissolving out of you,
And the stagnant tears.

I the great vein that leads
From the night to the source of you,
Which the sweet blood feeds.

New phase in the germ of you;
New sunny streams of blood
Washing you through.

You are born again of me.
I, Adam, from the veins of me
The Eve that is to be.

What has been long ago
Grows dimmer, we both forget,
We no longer know.

You are lovely, your face is soft
Like a flower in bud
On a mountain croft.

This is Noël for me.
To-night is a woman born
Of the man in me.

Rabbit Snared in the Night

Why do you spurt and sprottle
like that, bunny?
Why should I want to throttle
you, bunny?

Yes, bunch yourself between
my knees and lie still.
Lie on me with a hot, plumb, live weight,
heavy as a stone, passive,
yet hot, waiting.

What are you waiting for?
What are you waiting for?
What is the hot, plumb weight of your desire on me?
You have a hot, unthinkable desire of me, bunny.

What is that spark
glittering at me on the unutterable darkness
of your eye, bunny?
The finest splinter of a spark
that you throw off, straight on the tinder of my nerves!

It sets up a strange fire,
a soft, most unwarrantable burning
a bale-fire mounting, mounting up in me.

'Tis not of me, bunny.
It was you engendered it,
with that fine, demoniacal spark
you jetted off your eye at me.

I did not want it,
this furnace, this draught-maddened fire
which mounts up my arms
making them swell with turgid, ungovernable strength.

'Twas not *I* that wished it,
that my fingers should turn into these flames
avid and terrible
that they are at this moment.

It must have been *your* inbreathing, gaping desire
that drew this red gush in me;
I must be reciprocating *your* vacuous, hideous passion.

It must be the want in you
that has drawn this terrible draught of white fire
up my veins as up a chimney.

It must be you who desire
this intermingling of the black and monstrous fingers of Moloch
in the blood-jets of your throat.

Come, you shall have your desire,
since already I am implicated with you
in your strange lust.

Paradise Re-Entered

Through the strait gate of passion,
Between the bickering fire
Where flames of fierce love tremble
On the body of fierce desire:

To the intoxication,
The mind, fused down like a bead,
Flees in its agitation
The flames' stiff speed:

At last to calm incandescence,
Burned clean by remorseless hate,
Now, at the day's renascence
We approach the gate.

Now, from the darkened spaces
Of fear, and of frightened faces,
Death, in our awful embraces
Approached and passed by;

We near the flame-burnt porches
Where the brands of the angels, like torches
Whirl,—in these perilous marches
Pausing to sigh;

We look back on the withering roses,
The stars, in their sun-dimmed closes,
Where 'twas given us to repose us
Sure on our sanctity;

Beautiful, candid lovers,
Burnt out of our earthy covers,
We might have nestled like plovers
In the fields of eternity.

There, sure in sinless being,
All-seen, and then all-seeing,

In us life unto death agreeing,
We might have lain.

But we storm the angel-guarded
Gates of the long-discarded,
Garden, which God has hoarded
Against our pain.

The Lord of Hosts, and the Devil
Are left on Eternity's level
Field, and as victors we travel
To Eden home.

Back beyond good and evil
Return we. Eve dishevel
Your hair for the bliss-drenched revel
On our primal loam.

Spring Morning

Ah, through the open door
Is there an almond tree
Aflame with blossom!
    —Let us fight no more.

Among the pink and blue
Of the sky and the almond flowers
A sparrow flutters.
    —We have come through,

It is really spring!—See,
When he thinks himself alone
How he bullies the flowers.
    —Ah, you and me

How happy we'll be!—See him
He clouts the tufts of flowers
In his impudence.
    —But, did you dream

It would be so bitter? Never mind
It is finished, the spring is here.
And we're going to be summer-happy
    And summer-kind.

We have died, we have slain and been slain,
We are not our old selves any more.
I feel new and eager
    To start again.

It is gorgeous to live and forget.
And to feel quite new.
See the bird in the flowers?—he's making
    A rare to-do!

He thinks the whole blue sky
Is much less than the bit of blue egg
He's got in his nest—we'll be happy
      You and I, I and you.

With nothing to fight any more—
In each other, at least.
See, how gorgeous the world is
      Outside the door!

San Gaudenzio

Wedlock

I

Come, my little one, closer up against me,
Creep right up, with your round head pushed in my breast.

How I love all of you! Do you feel me wrap you
Up with myself and my warmth, like a flame round the wick?

And how I am not at all, except a flame that mounts off you.
Where I touch you, I flame into being;—but is it me, or you?

That round head pushed in my chest, like a nut in its socket,
And I the swift bracts that sheathe it: those breasts, those thighs and
    knees,

Those shoulders so warm and smooth: I feel that I
Am a sunlight upon them, that shines them into being.

But how lovely to be you! Creep closer in, that I am more.
I spread over you! How lovely, your round head, your arms,

Your breasts, your knees and feet! I feel that we
Are a bonfire of oneness, me flame flung leaping round you,
You the core of the fire, crept into me.

II

And oh, my little one, you whom I enfold,
How quaveringly I depend on you, to keep me alive,
Like a flame on a wick!

I, the man who enfolds you and holds you close,
How my soul cleaves to your bosom as I clasp you,
The very quick of my being!

Suppose you didn't want me! I should sink down
Like a light that has no sustenance
And sinks low.

Cherish me, my tiny one, cherish me who enfold you.
Nourish me, and endue me, I am only of you,
I am your issue.

How full and big like a robust, happy flame
When I enfold you, and you creep into me,
And my life is fierce at its quick
Where it comes off you!

III

My little one, my big one,
My bird, my brown sparrow in my breast.
My squirrel clutching in to me;
My pigeon, my little one, so warm
So close, breathing so still.

My little one, my big one,
I, who am so fierce and strong, enfolding you,
If you start away from my breast, and leave me,
How suddenly I shall go down into nothing
Like a flame that falls of a sudden.

And you will be before me, tall and towering,
And I shall be wavering uncertain
Like a sunken flame that grasps for support.

IV

But now I am full and strong and certain
With you there firm at the core of me
Keeping me.

How sure I feel, how warm and strong and happy
For the future! How sure the future is within me;
I am like a seed with a perfect flower enclosed.

I wonder what it will be,
What will come forth of us.
What flower, my love?

No matter, I am so happy,
I feel like a firm, rich, healthy root,
Rejoicing in what is to come.

How I depend on you utterly
My little one, my big one!
How everything that will be, will not be of me,
Nor of either of us,
But of both of us.

V

And think, there will something come forth from us.
We two, folded so small together,
There will something come forth from us.
Children, acts, utterance
Perhaps only happiness.

Perhaps only happiness will come forth from us.
Old sorrow, and new happiness.
Only that one newness.

But that is all I want.
And I am sure of that.
We are sure of that.

VI

And yet all the while you are you, you are not me.
And I am I, I am never you.
How awfully distinct and far off from each other's being we are!

Yet I am glad.
I am so glad there is always you beyond my scope,
Something that stands over,
Something I shall never be,
That I shall always wonder over, and wait for,
Look for like the breath of life as long as I live,
Still waiting for you, however old you are, and I am,
I shall always wonder over you, and look for you.

And you will always be with me.
I shall never cease to be filled with newness,
Having you near me.

History

The listless beauty of the hour
When snow fell on the apple trees
And the wood-ash gathered in the fire
And we faced our first miseries.

Then the sweeping sunshine of noon
When the mountains like chariot cars
Were ranked to blue battle—and you and I
Counted our scars.

And then in a strange, grey hour
We lay mouth to mouth, with your face
Under mine like a star on the lake,
And I covered the earth, and all space.

The silent, drifting hours
Of morn after morn
And night drifting up to the night
Yet no pathway worn.

Your life, and mine, my love
Passing on and on, the hate
Fusing closer and closer with love
Till at length they mate.

The Cearne

Song of a Man Who Has Come Through

Not I, not I, but the wind that blows through me!
A fine wind is blowing the new direction of Time.
If only I let it bear me, carry me, if only it carry me!
If only I am sensitive, subtle, oh, delicate, a winged gift!
If only, most lovely of all, I yield myself and am borrowed
By the fine, fine wind that takes its course through the chaos of the
        world
Like a fine, an exquisite chisel, a wedge-blade inserted;
If only I am keen and hard like the sheer tip of a wedge
Driven by invisible blows,
The rock will split, we shall come at the wonder, we shall find the
        Hesperides.

Oh, for the wonder that bubbles into my soul,
I would be a good fountain, a good well-head,
Would blur no whisper, spoil no expression.

What is the knocking?
What is the knocking at the door in the night?
It is somebody wants to do us harm.

No, no, it is the three strange angels.
Admit them, admit them.

One Woman to All Women

I don't care whether I am beautiful to you
        You other women.
Nothing of me that you see is my own;
A man balances, bone unto bone
Balances, everything thrown
        In the scale, you other women.

You may look and say to yourselves, I do
        Not show like the rest.
My face may not please you, nor my stature; yet if you knew
How happy I am, how my heart in the wind rings true
Like a bell that is chiming, each stroke as a stroke falls due,
        You other women:

You would draw your mirror towards you, you would wish
        To be different.
There's the beauty you cannot see, myself and him
Balanced in glorious equilibrium,
The swinging beauty of equilibrium,
        You other women.

There's this other beauty, the way of the stars
        You straggling women.
If you knew how I swerve in peace, in the equipoise
With the man, if you knew how my flesh enjoys
The swinging bliss no shattering ever destroys
        You other women:

You would envy me, you would think me wonderful
        Beyond compare;
You would weep to be lapsing on such harmony
As carries me, you would wonder aloud that he
Who is so strange should correspond with me
        Everywhere.

You see he is different, he is dangerous,
        Without pity or love.

And yet how his separate being liberates me
And gives me peace! You cannot see
How the stars are moving in surety
      Exquisite, high above.

We move without knowing, we sleep, and we travel on,
      You other women.
And this is beauty to me, to be lifted and gone
In a motion human inhuman, two and one
Encompassed, and many reduced to none,
      You other women.

Kensington

People

The great gold apples of night
Hang from the street's long bough
        Dripping their light
On the faces that drift below,
On the faces that drift and blow
Down the night-time, out of sight
        In the wind's sad sough.

The ripeness of these apples of night
Distilling over me
        Makes sickening the white
Ghost-flux of faces that hie
Them endlessly, endlessly by
Without meaning or reason why
        They ever should be.

Street Lamps

Gold, with an innermost speck
Of silver, singing afloat
    Beneath the night,
Like balls of thistle-down
Wandering up and down
Over the whispering town
    Seeking where to alight!

Slowly, above the street
Above the ebb of feet
    Drifting in flight;
Still, in the purple distance
The gold of their strange persistence
As they cross and part and meet
    And pass out of sight!

The seed-ball of the sun
Is broken at last, and done
    Is the orb of day.
Now to the separate ends
Seed after day-seed wends
    A separate way.

No sun will ever rise
Again on the wonted skies
    In the midst of the spheres.
The globe of the day, over-ripe,
Is shattered at last beneath the stripe
Of the wind, and its oneness veers
    Out myriad-wise.

Seed after seed after seed
Drifts over the town, in its need
    To sink and have done;
To settle at last in the dark,
To bury its weary spark
    Where the end is begun.

Darkness, and depth of sleep,
Nothing to know or to weep
    Where the seed sinks in
To the earth of the under-night
Where all is silent, quite
Still, and the darknesses steep
    Out all the sin.

"She Said As Well to Me"

She said as well to me: "Why are you ashamed?
That little bit of your chest that shows between
the gap of your shirt, why cover it up?
Why shouldn't your legs and your good strong thighs
be rough and hairy?—I'm glad they are like that.
You are shy, you silly, you silly shy thing.
Men are the shyest creatures, they never will come
out of their covers. Like any snake
slipping into its bed of dead leaves, you hurry into your clothes.
And I love you so! Straight and clean and all of a piece is the body
      of a man,
such an instrument, a spade, like a spear, or an oar,
such a joy to me—"
So she laid her hands and pressed them down my sides,
so that I began to wonder over myself, and what I was.

She said to me: "What an instrument, your body!
single and perfectly distinct from everything else!
What a tool in the hands of the Lord!
Only God could have brought it to its shape.
It feels as if his handgrasp, wearing you
had polished you and hollowed you,
hollowed this groove in your sides, grasped you under the breasts
and brought you to the very quick of your form,
subtler than an old, soft-worn fiddle-bow.

"When I was a child, I loved my father's riding-whip
that he used so often.
I loved to handle it, it seemed like a near part of him.
So I did his pens, and the jasper seal on his desk.
Something seemed to surge through me when I touched them.

"So it is with you, but here
The joy I feel!
God knows what I feel, but it is joy!
Look, you are clean and fine and singled out!
I admire you so, you are beautiful: this clean sweep of your sides, this
      firmness, this hard mould!

I would die rather than have it injured with one scar.
I wish I could grip you like the fist of the Lord,
and have you—"

So she said, and I wondered,
feeling trammelled and hurt.
It did not make me free.

Now I say to her: "No tool, no instrument, no God!
Don't touch me and appreciate me.
It is an infamy.
You would think twice before you touched a weasel on a fence
as it lifts its straight white throat.
Your hand would not be so flig and easy.
Nor the adder we saw asleep with her head on her shoulder,
curled up in the sunshine like a princess;
when she lifted her head in delicate, startled wonder
you did not stretch forward to caress her
though she looked rarely beautiful
and a miracle as she glided delicately away, with such dignity.
And the young bull in the field, with his wrinkled, sad face,
you are afraid if he rises to his feet,
though he is all wistful and pathetic, like a monolith, arrested, static.

"Is there nothing in me to make you hesitate?
I tell you there is all these.
And why should you overlook them in me?—"

New Heaven and Earth

I

And so I cross into another world
shyly and in homage linger for an invitation
from this unknown that I would trespass on.

I am very glad, and all alone in the world,
all alone, and very glad, in a new world
where I am disembarked at last.

I could cry with joy, because I am in the new world, just ventured in.
I could cry with joy, and quite freely, there is nobody to know.

And whosoever the unknown people of this unknown world may be
they will never understand my weeping for joy to be adventuring
      among them
because it will still be a gesture of the old world I am making
which they will not understand, because it is quite, quite foreign to them.

II

I was so weary of the world
I was so sick of it
everything was tainted with myself,
skies, trees, flowers, birds, water,
people, houses, streets, vehicles, machines,
nations, armies, war, peace-talking,
work, recreation, governing, anarchy,
it was all tainted with myself, I knew it all to start with
because it was all myself.

When I gathered flowers, I knew it was myself plucking my own
      flowering.
When I went in a train, I knew it was myself travelling by my own
      invention.
When I heard the cannon of the war, I listened with my own ears to
      my own destruction.

When I saw the torn dead, I knew it was my own torn dead body.
It was all me, I had done it all in my own flesh.

III

I shall never forget the maniacal horror of it all in the end
when everything was me, I knew it all already, I anticipated it all in
        my soul
because I was the author and the result
I was the God and the creation at once;
creator, I looked at my creation;
created, I looked at myself, the creator:
it was a maniacal horror in the end.

I was a lover, I kissed the woman I loved,
and God of horror, I was kissing also myself.
I was a father and a begetter of children,
and oh, oh horror, I was begetting and conceiving
in my own body.

IV

At last came death, sufficiency of death,
and that at last relieved me, I died.
I buried my beloved; it was good, I buried myself and was gone.
War came, and every hand raised to murder;
very good, very good, every hand raised to murder!
Very good, very good, I am a murderer!
It is good, I can murder and murder, and see them fall
the mutilated, horror-struck youths, a multitude
one on another, and then in clusters together
smashed, all oozing with blood, and burned in heaps
going up in a fœtid smoke to get rid of them
the murdered bodies of youths and men in heaps
and heaps and heaps and horrible reeking heaps
till it is almost enough, till I am reduced perhaps;
thousands and thousands of gaping, hideous foul dead
that are youths and men and me

being burned with oil, and consumed in corrupt thick smoke, that rolls
and taints and blackens the sky, till at last it is dark, dark as night, or
    death, or hell
and I am dead, and trodden to nought in the smoke-sodden tomb;
dead and trodden to nought in the sour black earth
of the tomb; dead and trodden to nought, trodden to nought.

V

God, but it is good to have died and been trodden out
trodden to nought in sour, dead earth
quite to nought
absolutely to nothing
nothing
nothing
nothing.

For when it is quite, quite nothing, then it is everything.
When I am trodden quite out, quite, quite out
every vestige gone, then I am here
risen, and setting my foot on another world
risen, accomplishing a resurrection
risen, not born again, but risen, body the same as before,
new beyond knowledge of newness, alive beyond life
proud beyond inkling or furthest conception of pride
living where life was never yet dreamed of, nor hinted at
here, in the other world, still terrestrial
myself, the same as before, yet unaccountably new.

VI

I, in the sour black tomb, trodden to absolute death
I put out my hand in the night, one night, and my hand
touched that which was verily not me
verily it was not me.
Where I had been was a sudden blaze
a sudden flaring blaze!
So I put my hand out further, a little further

and I felt that which was not I,
it verily was not I
it was the unknown.

Ha, I was a blaze leaping up!
I was a tiger bursting into sunlight.
I was greedy, I was mad for the unknown.
I, new-risen, resurrected, starved from the tomb
starved from a life of devouring always myself
now here was I, new-awakened, with my hand stretching out
and touching the unknown, the real unknown, the unknown unknown.

My God, but I can only say
I touch, I feel the unknown!
I am the first comer!

Cortes, Pisarro, Columbus, Cabot, they are nothing, nothing!
I am the first comer!
I am the discoverer!
I have found the other world!

The unknown, the unknown!
I am thrown upon the shore.
I am covering myself with the sand.
I am filling my mouth with the earth.
I am burrowing my body into the soil.
The unknown, the new world!

VII

It was the flank of my wife
I touched with my hand, I clutched with my hand
rising, new-awakened from the tomb!
It was the flank of my wife
whom I married years ago
at whose side I have lain for over a thousand nights
and all that previous while, she was I, she was I;
I touched her, it was I who touched and I who was touched.

Yet rising from the tomb, from the black oblivion
stretching out my hand, my hand flung like a drowned man's hand
    on a rock,
I touched her flank and knew I was carried by the current in death
over to the new world, and was climbing out on the shore,
risen, not to the old world, the old, changeless I, the old life,
wakened not to the old knowledge
but to a new earth, a new I, a new knowledge, a new world of time.

Ah no, I cannot tell you what it is, the new world
I cannot tell you the mad, astounded rapture of its discovery.
I shall be mad with delight before I have done,
and whosoever comes after will find me in the new world
a madman in rapture.

VIII

Green streams that flow from the innermost continent of the new world,
what are they?
Green and illumined and travelling for ever
dissolved with the mystery of the innermost heart of the continent
ery beyond knowledge or endurance, so sumptuous
out of the well-heads of the new world.—
The other, she too has strange green eyes!
White sands and fruits unknown and perfumes that never
can blow across the dark seas to our usual world!
And land that beats with a pulse!
And valleys that draw close in love!
And strange ways where I fall into oblivion of uttermost living!—
Also she who is the other has strange-mounded breasts and strange
    sheer slopes, and white levels.

Sightless and strong oblivion in utter life takes possession of me!
The unknown, strong current of life supreme
drowns me and sweeps me away and holds me down
to the sources of mystery, in the depths,
extinguishes there my risen resurrected life
and kindles it further at the core of utter mystery.

Greatham

Elysium

I have found a place of loneliness
Lonelier than Lyonesse
Lovelier than Paradise;

Full of sweet stillness
That no noise can transgress
Never a lamp distress.

The full moon sank in state.
I saw her stand and wait
For her watchers to shut the gate.

Then I found myself in a wonderland
All of shadow and of bland
Silence hard to understand.

I waited therefore; then I knew
The presence of the flowers that grew
Noiseless, their wonder noiseless blew.

And flashing kingfishers that flew
In sightless beauty, and the few
Shadows the passing wild-beast threw.

And Eve approaching over the ground
Unheard and subtle, never a sound
To let me know that I was found.

Invisible the hands of Eve
Upon me travelling to reeve
Me from the matrix, to relieve

Me from the rest! Ah terribly
Between the body of life and me
Her hands slid in and set me free.

Ah, with a fearful, strange detection
She found the source of my subjection
To the All, and severed the connection.

Delivered helpless and amazed
From the womb of the All, I am waiting, dazed
For memory to be erased.

Then I shall know the Elysium
That lies outside the monstrous womb
Of time from out of which I come.

Manifesto

I

A woman has given me strength and affluence.
Admitted!

All the rocking wheat of Canada, ripening now,
has not so much of strength as the body of one woman
sweet in ear, nor so much to give
though it feed nations.

Hunger is the very Satan.
The fear of hunger is Moloch, Belial, the horrible God.
It is a fearful thing to be dominated by the fear of hunger.

Not bread alone, not the belly nor the thirsty throat.
I have never yet been smitten through the belly, with the lack of bread,
no, nor even milk and honey.

The fear of the want of these things seems to be quite left out of me.
For so much, I thank the good generations of mankind.

II

And the sweet, constant, balanced heat
of the suave sensitive body, the hunger for this
has never seized me and terrified me.
Here again, man has been good in his legacy to us, in these two
      primary instances.

III

Then the dumb, aching, bitter, helpless need,
the pining to be initiated,
to have access to the knowledge that the great dead
have opened up for us, to know, to satisfy

the great and dominant hunger of the mind;
man's sweetest harvest of the centuries, sweet, printed books,
bright, glancing, exquisite corn of many a stubborn
glebe in the upturned darkness;
I thank mankind with passionate heart
that I just escaped the hunger for these,
that they were given when I needed them,
because I am the son of man.

I have eaten, and drunk, and warmed and clothed my body,
I have been taught the language of understanding,
I have chosen among the bright and marvellous books,
like any prince, such stores of the world's supply
were open to me, in the wisdom and goodness of man.
So far, so good.
Wise, good provision that makes the heart swell with love!

IV

But then came another hunger
very deep, and ravening;
the very body's body crying out
with a hunger more frightening, more profound
than stomach or throat or even the mind;
redder than death, more clamorous.

The hunger for the woman. Alas,
it is so deep a Moloch, ruthless and strong,
'tis like the unutterable name of the dread Lord,
not to be spoken aloud.
Yet there it is, the hunger which comes upon us,
which we must learn to satisfy with pure, real satisfaction;
or perish, there is no alternative.

I thought it was woman, indiscriminate woman,
mere female adjunct of what I was.
Ah, that was torment hard enough
and a thing to be afraid of,
a threatening, torturing, phallic Moloch.

A woman fed that hunger in me at last.
What many women cannot give, one woman can;
so I have known it.

She stood before me like riches that were mine.
Even then, in the dark, I was tortured, ravening, unfree,
Ashamed, and shameful, and vicious.
A man is so terrified of strong hunger;
and this terror is the root of all cruelty.
She loved me, and stood before me, looking to me.
How could I look, when I was mad? I looked sideways, furtively,
being mad with voracious desire.

V

This comes right at last.
When a man is rich, he loses at last the hunger fear.
I lost at last the fierceness that fears it will starve.
I could put my face at last between her breasts
and know that they were given for ever
that I should never starve
never perish;
I had eaten of the bread that satisfies
and my body's body was appeased,
there was peace and richness,
fulfilment.

Let them praise desire who will,
but only fulfilment will do,
real fulfilment, nothing short.
It is our ratification
our heaven, as a matter of fact.
Immortality, the heaven, is only a projection of this strange but actual
        fulfilment,
here in the flesh.

So, another hunger was supplied,
and for this I have to thank one woman,

not mankind, for mankind would have prevented me;
but one woman,
and these are my red-letter thanksgivings.

VI

To be, or not to be, is still the question.
This ache for being is the ultimate hunger.
And for myself, I can say "almost, almost, oh, very nearly."
Yet something remains.
Something shall not always remain.
For the main already is fulfilment.

What remains in me, is to be known even as I know.
I know her now: or perhaps, I know my own limitation against her.

Plunging as I have done, over, over the brink
I have dropped at last headlong into nought, plunging upon sheer
        hard extinction;
I have come, as it were, not to know,
died, as it were; ceased from knowing; surpassed myself.
What can I say more, except that I know what it is to surpass myself?

It is a kind of death which is not death.
It is going a little beyond the bounds.
How can one speak, where there is a dumbness on one's mouth?
I suppose, ultimately she is all beyond me,
she is all not-me, ultimately.
It is that that one comes to.
A curious agony, and a relief, when I touch that which is not me in
        any sense,
it wounds me to death with my own not-being; definite, inviolable
        limitation,
and something beyond, quite beyond, if you understand what that means.
It is the major part of being, this having surpassed oneself,
this having touched the edge of the beyond, and perished, yet not
        perished.

VII

I want her though, to take the same from me.
She touches me as if I were herself, her own.
She has not realized yet, that fearful thing, that I am the other,
she thinks we are all of one piece.
It is painfully untrue.

I want her to touch me at last, ah, on the root and quick of my darkness
and perish on me, as I have perished on her.

Then, we shall be two and distinct, we shall have each our separate being.
And that will be pure existence, real liberty.
Till then, we are confused, a mixture, unresolved, unextricated one from
    the other.
It is in pure, unutterable resolvedness, distinction of being, that one is
    free,
not in mixing, merging, not in similarity.
When she has put her hand on my secret, darkest sources, the darkest
    outgoings,
when it has struck home to her, like a death, "this is *him*!"
she has no part in it, no part whatever,
it is the terrible *other*,
when she knows the fearful *other flesh*, ah, darkness unfathomable
    and fearful, contiguous and concrete,
when she is slain against me, and lies in a heap like one outside the
    house,
when she passes away as I have passed away
being pressed up against the *other*,
then I shall be glad, I shall not be confused with her,
I shall be cleared, distinct, single as if burnished in silver,
having no adherence, no adhesion anywhere,
one clear, burnished, isolated being, unique,
and she also, pure, isolated, complete,
two of us, unutterably distinguished, and in unutterable conjunction.

Then we shall be free, freer than angels, ah, perfect.

VIII

After that, there will only remain that all men detach themselves and
        become unique,
that we are all detached, moving in freedom more than the angels,
conditioned only by our own pure single being,
having no laws but the laws of our own being.

Every human being will then be like a flower, untrammelled.
Every movement will be direct.
Only to be will be such delight, we cover our faces when we think of it
lest our faces betray us to some untimely fiend.

Every man himself, and therefore, a surpassing singleness of mankind.
The blazing tiger will spring upon the deer, undimmed,
the hen will nestle over her chickens,
we shall love, we shall hate,
but it will be like music, sheer utterance,
issuing straight out of the unknown,
the lightning and the rainbow appearing in us unbidden, unchecked,
like ambassadors.

We shall not look before and after.
We shall *be, now*.
We shall know in full.
We, the mystic NOW.

Zennor

Autumn Rain

The plane leaves
fall black and wet
on the lawn;

The cloud sheaves
in heaven's fields set
droop and are drawn

in falling seeds of rain;
the seed of heaven
on my face

falling—I hear again
like echoes even
that softly pace

Heaven's muffled floor,
the winds that tread
out all the grain
of tears, the store
harvested
in the sheaves of pain

caught up aloft:
the sheaves of dead
men that are slain

now winnowed soft
on the floor of heaven;
manna invisible

of all the pain
here to us given;
finely divisible
falling as rain.

Frost Flowers

It is not long since, here among all these folk
in London, I should have held myself
of no account whatever,
but should have stood aside and made them way
thinking that they, perhaps,
had more right than I—for who was I?

Now I see them just the same, and watch them.
But of what account do I hold them?

Especially the young women. I look at them
as they dart and flash
before the shops, like wagtails on the edge of a pool.

If I pass them close, or any man,
like sharp, slim wagtails they flash a little aside
pretending to avoid us; yet all the time
calculating.

They think that we adore them—alas, would it were true!
Probably they think all men adore them,
howsoever they pass by.

What is it, that, from their faces fresh as spring,
such fair, fresh, alert, first-flower faces,
like lavender crocuses, snowdrops, like Roman hyacinths,
scyllas and yellow-haired hellebore, jonquils, dim anemones,
even the sulphur auriculas,
flowers that come first from the darkness, and feel cold to the touch,
flowers scentless or pungent, ammoniacal almost;
what is it, that, from the faces of the fair young women
comes like a pungent scent, a vibration beneath
that startles me, alarms me, stirs up a repulsion?

They are the issue of acrid winter, these first-flower young women;
their scent is lacerating and repellant,
it smells of burning snow, of hot-ache,

of earth, winter-pressed, strangled in corruption;
it is the scent of the fiery-cold dregs of corruption,
when destruction soaks through the mortified, decomposing earth,
and the last fires of dissolution burn in the bosom of the ground.

They are the flowers of ice-vivid mortification,
thaw-cold, ice-corrupt blossoms,
with a loveliness I loathe;
for what kind of ice-rotten, hot-aching heart must they need to root in!

Craving for Spring

I wish it were spring in the world.

Let it be spring!
Come, bubbling, surging tide of sap!
Come, rush of creation!
Come, life! surge through this mass of mortification!
Come, sweep away these exquisite, ghastly first-flowers,
which are rather last-flowers!
Come, thaw down their cool portentousness, dissolve them:
snowdrops, straight, death-veined exhalations of white and purple
          crocuses,
flowers of the penumbra, issue of corruption, nourished in
          mortification,
jets of exquisite finality;
Come, spring, make havoc of them!

I trample on the snowdrops, it gives me pleasure to tread down the
          jonquils,
to destroy the chill Lent lilies;
for I am sick of them, their faint-bloodedness,
slow-blooded, icy-fleshed, portentous.

I want the fine, kindling wine-sap of spring,
gold, and of inconceivably fine, quintessential brightness,
rare almost as beams, yet overwhelmingly potent,
strong like the greatest force of world-balancing.

This is the same that picks up the harvest of wheat
and rocks it, tons of grain, on the ripening wind;
the same that dangles the globe-shaped pleiads of fruit
temptingly in mid-air, between a playful thumb and finger;
oh, and suddenly, from out [of nowhere, whirls the pear-bloom,
upon us, and apple- and almond- and apricot- and quince-blossom,
storms and cumulus clouds of all imaginable blossom
about our bewildered faces,
though we do not worship.

I wish it were spring
cunningly blowing on the fallen sparks, odds and ends of the old,
        scattered fire,
and kindling shapely little conflagrations
curious long-legged foals, and wide-eared calves, and naked sparrow-
        bubs.

I wish that spring
would start the thundering traffic of feet
new feet on the earth, beating with impatience.

I wish it were spring, thundering
delicate, tender spring.
I wish these brittle, frost-lovely flowers of passionate, mysterious
        corruption
were not yet to come still more from the still-flickering discontent.

Oh, in the spring, the bluebell bows him down for very exuberance,
exulting with secret warm excess,
bowed down with his inner magnificence!

Oh, yes, the gush of spring is strong enough
to toss the globe of earth like a ball on a water-jet
dancing sportfully;
as you see a tiny celluloid ball tossing on a squint of water
for men to shoot at, penny-a-time, in a booth at a fair.

The gush of spring is strong enough
to play with the globe of earth like a ball on a fountain;
At the same time it opens the tiny hands of the hazel
with such infinite patience.

The power of the rising, golden, all-creative sap could take the earth
and heave it off among the stars, into the invisible;
the same sets the throstle at sunset on a bough
singing against the blackbird;
comes out in the hesitating tremor of the primrose,
and betrays its candour in the round white strawberry flower,
is dignified in the foxglove, like a Red-Indian brave.

Ah come, come quickly, spring!
Come and lift us towards our culmination, we myriads;
we who have never flowered, like patient cactuses.
Come and lift us to our end, to blossom, bring us to our summer
we who are winter-weary in the winter of the world.
Come making the chaffinch nests hollow and cosy,
come and soften the willow buds till they are puffed and furred,
then blow them over with gold.
Come and cajole the gawky colt's-foot flowers.

Come quickly, and vindicate us
against too much death.
Come quickly, and stir the rotten globe of the world from within,
burst it with germination, with world anew.
Come now, to us, your adherents, who cannot flower from the ice.
All the world gleams with the lilies of Death the Unconquerable,
but come, give us our turn.
Enough of the virgins and lilies, of passionate, suffocating perfume of
    corruption,
no more narcissus perfume, lily harlots, the blades of sensation
piercing the flesh to blossom of death.
Have done, have done with this shuddering, delicious business
of thrilling ruin in the flesh, of pungent passion, of rare, death-edged
    ecstasy.
Give us our turn, give us a chance, let our hour strike,
O soon, soon!
Let the darkness turn violet with rich dawn.
Let the darkness be warmed, warmed through to a ruddy violet,
incipient purpling towards summer in the world of the heart of man.

Are the violets already here!
Show me! I tremble so much to hear it, that even now
on the threshold of spring, I fear I shall die.
Show me the violets that are out.

Oh, if it be true, and the living darkness of the blood of man is
    purpling with violets,
if the violets are coming out from under the rack of men, winter-
    rotten and fallen

we shall have spring.
Pray not to die on this Pisgah blossoming with violets.
Pray to live through.

If you catch a whiff of violets from the darkness of the shadow of man
it will be spring in the world,
it will be spring in the world of the living;
wonderment organising itself, heralding itself with the violets,
stirring of new seasons.

Ah, do not let me die on the brink of such anticipation!
Worse, let me not deceive myself.

Zennor

Appendix

containing three poems added to the section devoted to
Look! We Have Come Through! in Lawrence's *Collected Poems* (1937),
and two poems excluded from the first edition at the request of
the publisher.

Bei Hennef

The little river twittering in the twilight,
The wan, wondering look of the pale sky,
    This is almost bliss.

And everything shut up and gone to sleep,
All the troubles and anxieties and pain
    Gone under the twilight.

Only the twilight now, and the soft "Sh!" of the river
    That will last for ever.

And at last I know my love for you is here;
I can see it all, it is whole like the twilight,
It is large, so large, I could not see it before,
Because of the little lights and flickers and interruptions,
    Troubles, anxieties and pains.

    You are the call and I am the answer,
    You are the wish, and I the fulfilment,
    You are the night, and I the day.
        What else? it is perfect enough.
        It is perfectly complete,
        You and I,
        What more—?

Strange, how we suffer in spite of this.

Hennef am Rhein

Everlasting Flowers

For a Dead Mother

Who do you think stands watching
    The snow-tops shining rosy
In heaven, now that the darkness
    Takes all but the tallest posy?

Who then sees the two-winged
    Boat down there, all alone
And asleep on the snow's last shadow,
    Like a moth on a stone?

The olive-leaves, light as gad-flies,
    Have all gone dark, gone black.
And now in the dark my soul to you
    Turns back.

To you, my little darling,
    To you, out of Italy.
For what is loveliness, my love,
    Save you have it with me!

So, there's an oxen wagon
    Comes darkly into sight:
A man with a lantern, swinging
    A little light.

What does he see, my darling
    Here by the darkened lake?
Here, in the sloping shadow
    The mountains make?

He says not a word, but passes,
    Staring at what he sees.
What ghost of us both do you think he saw
    Under the olive trees?

All the things that are lovely—
    The things you never knew—
I wanted to gather them one by one
    And bring them to you.

But never now, my darling
    Can I gather the mountain-tips
From the twilight like half-shut lilies
    To hold to your lips.

And never the two-winged vessel
    That sleeps below on the lake
Can I catch like a moth between my hands
    For you to take.

But hush, I am not regretting:
    It is far more perfect now.
I'll whisper the ghostly truth to the world
    And tell them how

I know you here in the darkness,
    How you sit in the throne of my eyes
At peace, and look out of the windows
    In glad surprise.

Lago di Garda

Coming Awake

When I woke, the lake-lights were quivering on the wall,
    The sunshine swam in a shoal across and across,
And a hairy, big bee hung over the primulas
    In the window, his body black fur, and the sound of him cross.

There was something I ought to remember: and yet
    I did not remember. Why should I? The running lights
And the airy primulas, oblivious
    Of the impending bee—they were fair enough sights.

Song of a Man Who Is Loved

Between her breasts is my home, between her breasts.
Three sides set on me space and fear, but the fourth side rests
Sure and a tower of strength, 'twixt the walls of her breasts.

Having known the world so long, I have never confessed
How it impresses me, how hard and compressed
Rocks seem, and earth, and air uneasy, and waters still ebbing west.

All things on the move, going their own little ways, and all
Jostling, people touching and talking and making small
Contacts and bouncing off again, bounce! bounce like a ball!

My flesh is weary with bounce and gone again!—
My eyes are weary with words that bounce on them, and then
Bounce off again, meaning nothing. Assertions! Assertions! stones,
       women and men!

Between her breasts is my home, between her breasts.
Three sides set on me chaos and bounce, but the fourth side rests
Sure on a haven of peace, between the mounds of her breasts.

I am that I am, and no more than that: but so much
I am, nor will I be bounced out of it. So at last I touch
All that I am-not in softness, sweet softness, for she is such.

And the chaos that bounces and rattles like shrapnel, at least
Has for me a door into peace, warm dawn in the east
Where her bosom softens towards me, and the turmoil has ceased.

So I hope I shall spend eternity
With my face down buried between her breasts;
And my still heart full of security,
And my still hands full of her breasts.

Revised version, as printed in the *Collected Poems* (1928)

Song of a Man That Is Loved

Between her breasts is my home, between her breasts.
Three sides set on me space and fear, but the fourth side rests,
Warm in a city of strength, between her breasts.

All day long I am busy and happy at my work
I need not glance over my shoulder in fear of the terrors that lurk
Behind. I am fortified, I am glad at my work.

I need not look after my soul; beguile my fear
With prayer, I need only come home each night to find the dear
Door on the latch, and shut myself in, shut out fear.

I need only come home each night and lay
My face between her breasts;
And what of good I have given the day, my peace attests.

And what I have failed in, what I have wronged
Comes up unnamed from her body and surely
Silent tongued I am ashamed.

And I hope to spend eternity
With my face down-buried between her breasts
And my still heart full of security
And my still hands full of her breasts

(Original 1917 version)

Meeting Among the Mountains

The little pansies by the road have turned
Away their purple faces and their gold,
And evening has taken all the bees from the thyme,
And all the scent is shed away by the cold.

Against the hard and pale blue evening sky
The mountain's new-dropped summer snow is clear
Glistening in steadfast stillness: like transcendent
Clean pain sending on us a chill down here.

Christ on the Cross!—his beautiful young man's body
Has fallen dead upon the nails, and hangs
White and loose at last, with all the pain
Drawn on his mouth, eyes broken at last by his pangs.

And slowly down the mountain road, belated,
A bullock wagon comes; so I am ashamed
To gaze any more at the Christ, whom the mountain snows
Whitely confront; I wait on the grass, am lamed.

The breath of the bullock stains the hard, chill air,
The band is across its brow, and it scarcely seems
To draw the load, so still and slow it moves,
While the driver on the shaft sits crouched in dreams.

Surely about his sunburnt face is something
That vexes me with wonder. He sits so still
Here among all this silence, crouching forward,
Dreaming and letting the bullock take its will.

I stand aside on the grass to let them go;
—And Christ, I have met his accusing eyes again,
The brown eyes black with misery and hate, that look
Full in my own, and the torment starts again.

One moment the hate leaps at me standing there,
One moment I see the stillness of agony,

Something frozen in the silence that dare not be
Loosed, one moment the darkness frightens me.

Then among the averted pansies, beneath the high
White peaks of snow, at the foot of the sunken Christ
I stand in a chill of anguish, trying to say
The joy I bought was not too highly priced.

But he has gone, motionless, hating me,
Living as the mountains do, because they are strong,
With a pale, dead Christ on the crucifix of his heart,
And breathing the frozen memory of his wrong.

Still in his nostrils the frozen breath of despair,
And heart like a cross that bears dead agony
Of naked love, clenched in his fists the shame,
And in his belly the smouldering hate of me.

And I, as I stand in the cold, averted flowers,
Feel the shame-wounds in his hands pierce through my own,
And breathe despair that turns my lungs to stone
And know the dead Christ weighing on my bone.

Text as published in Georgian Poetry 1913–1915. *Reprinted in Frieda Lawrence's memoir* Not I, But the Wind *(1934), and also in the Ark Press edition of* Look! We Have Come Through! *(1957).*

www.ingramcontent.com/pod-product-compliance
Lightning Source LLC
Chambersburg PA
CBHW031154160426
43193CB00008B/365